Copyright 2020 Baburaj V Nair
All rights are reserved
Cochin, Kerala, India
June, 2020

Published by Kindle Direct Publishing

ISBN: 9798651707690

This collection of poems is dedicated to
all those people who served and
saved other people, during
pandemic times in the year 2020

<u>PREFACE</u>

When the new year got celebrated, none of us believed that in a month or two, the entire world is going to stagger into an unknown road due to a virus known as new Corona 2019.

Like a drunkard teetering on a street, oblivious of what is happening to him or around him, this virus has impacted each one of us, in different variations, and is currently threatening the otherwise "harmonial" life we had, so far.

"Harmonial" because, we never lived our life in harmony, though we always wanted to have a peaceful life. Paradoxically, whether it is work-life, family life, or social life, most of us never lived in harmony, in its true sense. Perceived wealth dictated our life of illusion, vehemently disagreeing to our own intrinsic beliefs.

At this make belief world, I wanted to express my feelings, which may echo through some of your emotions too.

In this collection, I have saluted people who are central to help others during this pandemic time – nurses (the butterfly), moustache (police force), doctors (the magic wand), using the term "the little spoiled brat" for the virus. I also tried to provide expression to lives of farmers and the incidents happened in Kerala (the God's Own Country), and in USA to express my anguish towards the injustice spreading in the Society.

Many well-wishers have helped me in this journey of expression, and with a sense of gratitude to each one of them, I submit my "mirror: a reflective journey through pandemic times" to those people, who have a courage of conviction, who still values virtues of moral courage.

Baburaj
Cochin, Kerala, India.

June 8, 2020

CONTENTS

THE UNKNOWN ROAD

They seem to be in a shock,
Which they do not want to express
They continue to want to believe,
That all will be okay in a couple of months,
And all will bounce back.

The environment indicated differently
Pointers were saying another story: A story of despair.
Why are they acting paradoxically?

Because I believe,
Nobody wants to walk on the unknown path
And be a trend setter.

Nobody wants to walk on the unknown path,
As the path will require truthfulness,
Which is "unknown" to most:
"If I do, will others do?
 If not, why should I?"

Nobody wants to walk on the unknown path,
As the path is full of building relationship
All the way across.
How can I reach out to them,
Whom I did not, hitherto.

Nobody wants to walk on the unknown path
Why should they set forth a journey,
When the destination is not clear?

Forgetting that all of them started their journey
When the road they took was unknown to them.

What they are today
Was because of the risk they took then,
The dream they shared with others,
Who dared to dream together.

Therefore, believe in self and others again.
The road will be clearer
When we take the sojourn together
Be hopeful, for a better tomorrow,
A tomorrow of collaboration and togetherness
While keeping one another safe.

May 19, 2020

THE BEAMING SUN

The beaming sun's smile
Touched my heart,
It was not hot, but warm
Stirring my soul.

The wobbling hut,
Adjacent to the pier
Reminded me the life so far –
Burned out, and battered
From all sides.

And the sun afar
Touching my body
In the wee hours of morning
Stirred hopefulness for tomorrow
Within me.

I was sure that the rays of hope will take me
Much further, and meaningfully
Than what I did till now.
If only, I am ready to take the risk.

Looking at the rays beaming
Through the cluster of trees,
Caressing my inner self
A hope of togetherness
A ray of happiness
Gave me a sense of self assurance
As the epitome of love
Caressing the little kid on her lap

June 4, 2020

THE DRUNKARD

Like the fire burning through the forest,
Like a drunkard wobbling
It ran amok in the lives of people
Around the globe

The tiny virus, playful,
Not knowing the catastrophe
It is making in the society
Among kith and kin

Like a drunkard
It staggered through the streets

The dwarf,
Waited with patience
And played havoc with
Only people who played with him

People who know him –
His waywardness
Stayed away from him.
But some people enjoyed playing with him
Not knowing what is in store
And they paid the price with their lives

Since all around him was oblivious
The little one,
Moved around with an audacity
With others found difficult to counter

People, around the globe, believed
That the day is not so far
When the little spoiled brat
Will realize his pitiful life
And stop his tantrums,
For the betterment of mankind.

June 1, 2020

DISTANCE

 "Back off"
With his eyes glowing in red
It stared at the people behind

People who know the danger
Of hitting him from behind
Kept the distance.
Knowing fully well,
That one knock is enough
To knock the life out of them

Some people where in a hurry
To move fast -
To go ahead of him
To tease him
And they perished

I, like many, believed in him
Kept the distance
Allowed him to pass by
To move forward

While passing by,
The giant gave me a smirk
And a wink
"You know the rule, baby.
You will survive".

May 15, 2020

THE BUTTERFLY

She moved around
With eyes of innocence
Hovering around each bed
With a sense of duty

The colourful, beautiful, skinny
Waited at each bed
Taking care of their happiness
Not bothering about her own health

Spreading her wings of peace
Nipping the "little playful spoiled brat"
With her needle
She gave a sense of courage
To all around her

Entrusting our lives in her skilful hands,
We waited with bated breath
Saluting her spirit of love in silent.

March 10, 2020

THE MOUSTACHE

The spoiled brat, born in a lab
Was oblivious of his tantrums
Impacting the society around him.

The "little brat" depopulated villages
Made people scamper for their lives
But "the moustache" stood his ground
Giving solace to his people.

He sported the moustache, "walrus",
Showing the courage
And serving his people with dignity

Hither and thither,
Wherever he was needed,
Diligently he worked
Around his people –
Old or young, destitute or otherwise.

Bold, and unflinching
His mere presence anywhere
Gave people a sense of reassurance
With an iron fist and walrus moustache
With firmness and fairness,

He guarded the gates
Of his village along with his brethren
Spoiling the games of the "little brat"

March 25, 2020

THE MAGIC WAND

She stood there with Herald's wand
Weaving a magic
Around her people
Healing the "sleeping" people,
Making it gentle for the unhealed

Serpents coiled around her wand
Balancing between the hope and despair
The wings spread across the land
She encircled – to take care of the needy.
Her presence with "two strings"
Around her neck – as a necklace
Gave a sense of re-assurance
A sense of hopefulness
For all who came across her

But, when one of the serpents
Encircled her body, she did not flinch
She fought with the serpent
With an alacrity of a mongoose

Both were tired –
the mongoose and the serpent -
At the end of the fight

People watching the fight – in utter despair
Found both falling on the ground -
Like a dry leaf falling from the branch of a tree.
They prayed for her to come back alive.

Few minutes later, they saw the mongoose
Alive and the serpent dead.
They saw a slight movement of her body
All of them rejoiced,
As their hope returned.

April 1, 2020

BARBARISM

While the spoiled brat
Played "ping-pong" and "hide and seek"
With people around the globe
A few hooligans, "played" with an elephant
In "Gods Own Country".

Trusting people earnestly,
She with a baby in womb,
Ate the fruits given to her
Not knowing
The darkness befalling on her.
The poisoned fruit, cracked inside her
Killing her child instantly
Bearing the pain of loss
She stood in water to quench
Her excruciating pain

Agonised, she died
The forest ranger,
Who saw this barbaric act
Cried in anguish
Shouting aloud
Who can do such a heinous act
Who is sane?
That too in the "God's Own Country".

The hooligan did not kill only her
But destroyed faith in mankind
Sabotaged kindness
And brought us back into the world
Of darkness.

Is mere punishment will deter such actions?

June 4, 2020

THE FARMER

The soil and the land
Stood with him and his family
In thick and thin times

Ploughing his land to ready for sowing
Making his land more fertile
He and his family dreamt of a better life
A life full of merriment –
Having enough to eat, cloth, shelter, and educate his children
The money, he owed to the landlord
Was a burden
He never could carry by himself
He sought help –
Alas, nobody came to his help

Like, thunder along with lightening
Hitting on his dilapidated hut,
The "spoiled brat" came and
Hit the poor farmer directly.

With a feverish body, he went
To the "angel with the Herald's wand"
In the village

Putting her best smile on face
She cared for his sickness,
With all sincerity and warmth
But here too, he could not sustain.

The "eternal truth" visited a few days later,
To take him to the abode of God.

Unable to sustain life after him
Landsharks bating their breath
Around the corner,
The whole family followed the farmer
Putting the entire village
Into a "torrential rain" of sadness.

When will we have an equitable life
In this pompous world?

May 14, 2020

THE VOLCANO

It smouldered within
Waiting for the imbalance
To erupt out.

The "eternal enemy" was not knowing
Which colour of skin, he was taking.
But the colour was black,
And the simmering heat
Started overflowing on the street.

Eons have lapsed
On the unobtrusive, invisibly felt
Caste, creed, and colours
Differentiating the mankind.

Who is superior –
Race, creed, or colour?
Or expression of humanity?
Who is inferior –
Race, creed, or colour?
Or the crestfallen face and
An empty stomach?

Who defines our life
Superior or inferior; Rich or Poor?
When did we lost our rights
To own our own life –
A life of freedom and purpose?

Doing a wrong thing –
Even if barbaric –
Is not a crime to be ashamed by the society,
As only a few misguided, barbaric people
Did such injustice to their brethren.

But, not having a sense of remorse
The "powers that be"
Siding with the injustice
Was the biggest shame for the society

If only the "powers in the higher echelons"
Can act with a sense of repentance
With a value of togetherness, and
If only they appreciate the truth of life,
Will the volcano erupt?

June 5, 2020.